EXPLORING COUNTRIES
Chile

by Lisa Owings

BELLWETHER MEDIA • MINNEAPOLIS, MN

Note to Librarians, Teachers, and Parents:

Blastoff! Readers are carefully developed by literacy experts and combine standards-based content with developmentally appropriate text.

Level 1 provides the most support through repetition of high-frequency words, light text, predictable sentence patterns, and strong visual support.

Level 2 offers early readers a bit more challenge through varied simple sentences, increased text load, and less repetition of high-frequency words.

Level 3 advances early-fluent readers toward fluency through increased text and concept load, less reliance on visuals, longer sentences, and more literary language.

Level 4 builds reading stamina by providing more text per page, increased use of punctuation, greater variation in sentence patterns, and increasingly challenging vocabulary.

Level 5 encourages children to move from "learning to read" to "reading to learn" by providing even more text, varied writing styles, and less familiar topics.

Whichever book is right for your reader, Blastoff! Readers are the perfect books to build confidence and encourage a love of reading that will last a lifetime!

This edition first published in 2012 by Bellwether Media, Inc.

No part of this publication may be reproduced in whole or in part without written permission of the publisher. For information regarding permission, write to Bellwether Media, Inc., Attention: Permissions Department, 5357 Penn Avenue South, Minneapolis, MN 55419.

Library of Congress Cataloging-in-Publication Data
Owings, Lisa.
 Chile / by Lisa Owings.
     p. cm. – (Exploring countries) (Blastoff! readers)
 Summary: "Developed by literacy experts for students in grades three through seven, this book introduces young readers to the geography and culture of Chile"–Provided by publisher.
 Includes bibliographical references and index.
 ISBN 978-1-60014-617-6 (hardcover : alk. paper)
 1. Chile–Juvenile literature. I. Title.
 F3058.5.O95 2012
 983–dc22
                                          2011002223

Text copyright © 2012 by Bellwether Media, Inc. BLASTOFF! READERS and associated logos are trademarks and/or registered trademarks of Bellwether Media, Inc. SCHOLASTIC, CHILDREN'S PRESS, and associated logos are trademarks and/or registered trademarks of Scholastic Inc.

Printed in the United States of America, North Mankato, MN.

Contents

Where Is Chile?	4
The Land	6
Torres del Paine	8
Wildlife	10
The People	12
Daily Life	14
Going to School	16
Working	18
Playing	20
Food	22
Holidays	24
Easter Island	26
Fast Facts	28
Glossary	30
To Learn More	31
Index	32

Where Is Chile?

Peru

Bolivia

Chile

Argentina

Pacific Ocean

Santiago

Chiloé Island

Tierra del Fuego

Did you know?
A sailor named Alexander Selkirk was deserted on a Chilean island in 1704. He lived there alone until 1709. The book *Robinson Crusoe* was likely inspired by Selkirk's story.

Chile is a long, skinny country that runs along the southwestern coast of South America. It is over 2,700 miles (4,345 kilometers) long and covers 291,933 square miles (756,102 square kilometers). Peru and Bolivia are its northern neighbors. To the east lies Argentina. The Pacific Ocean washes onto Chile's western shore. Easter Island, Chiloé Island, and much of Tierra del Fuego are part of Chile. Santiago, Chile's capital, lies in the center of the country.

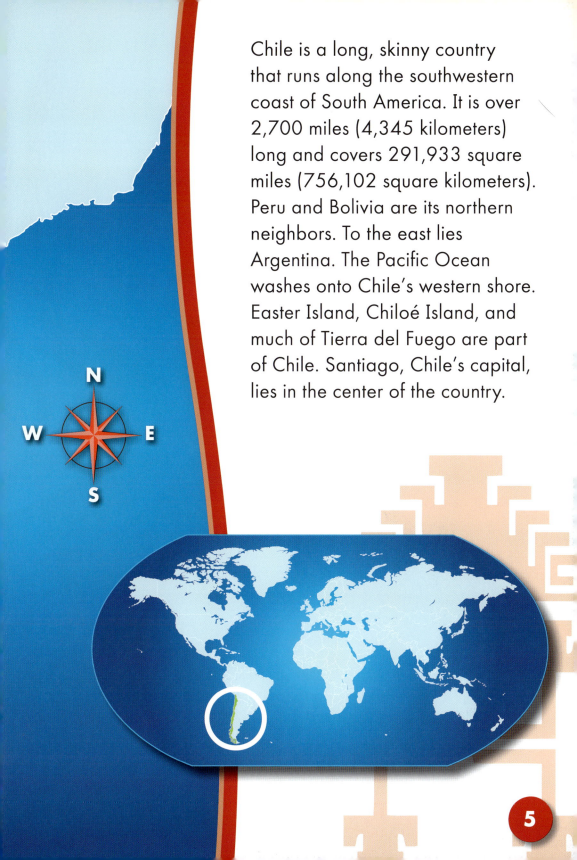

The Land

Atacama Desert

fun fact

The seasons in Chile are the opposite of the seasons in the United States. Summer begins in December and winter starts in June.

Chile's landscape varies greatly from north to south. The Atacama Desert covers northern Chile. It is the driest place in the world. Unlike many deserts, the Atacama is cool during the day. The land in central Chile receives a lot of rain. The damp soil is good for growing crops.

Southern Chile is cold, wet, and windy. The rugged land splits into hundreds of **fjords** and islands. **Glaciers** flow over parts of southern Chile. They feed lakes or spill into the ocean. The snow-covered Andes Mountains rise along Chile's eastern border. **Cape** Horn's rocky cliffs mark the southernmost point of both Chile and South America.

Torres del Paine

Chile's Torres del Paine is one of the most beautiful national parks in the world. **Tourists** come to see its jagged mountains, blue glaciers, and clear lakes. The park is named for three sharp rock towers that rise up to 8,000 feet (2,438 meters) into the sky. These towers are mountain peaks in the Cordillera del Paine. West of these mountains, glaciers feed cold lakes and streams.

Torres del Paine National Park has many trails for hikers and campers. These trails attract over 100,000 visitors per year. The most popular trail is in the shape of a "W." It winds through the mountains, along the shores of several lakes, and out onto the surface of Grey Glacier.

fun fact

Grey Glacier is the largest glacier in Torres del Paine National Park. It is almost 12 miles (20 kilometers) long and 4 miles (7 kilometers) wide!

Wildlife

pudú

flamingo

Darwin's frog

fun fact
The Darwin's frog lives in streams throughout Chile's forests. This frog grows up inside its dad's mouth!

Chile is home to a variety of animals. A few of the only animals that can survive in the Atacama Desert are lizards, scorpions, and gray foxes. South of the desert, chinchillas, viscachas, and other **rodents** scurry across the plains. Their predators include pumas and Andean wolves.

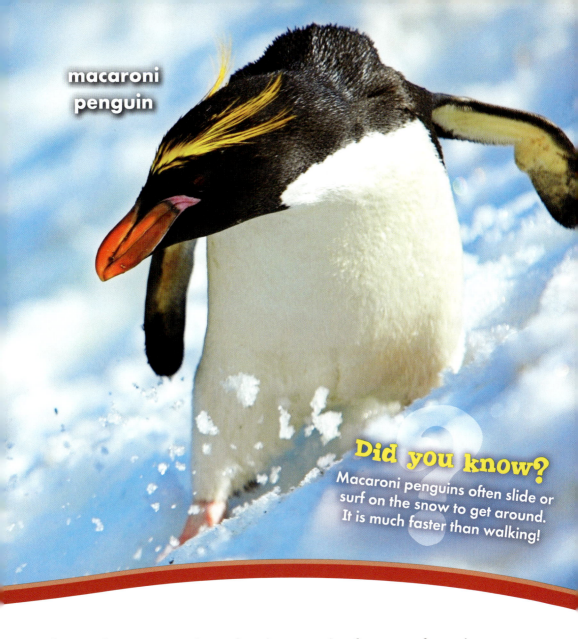

macaroni penguin

Did you know?
Macaroni penguins often slide or surf on the snow to get around. It is much faster than walking!

The pudú is a tiny deer that lives in the forests of southern Chile. At just over 12 inches (30 centimeters) tall, it is the smallest deer in the world! In the mountains, guanacos and cougars roam the land. Parrots and flamingoes make their homes in northern and central Chile. Off the coast, seals and penguins swim with blue whales, the largest animals on Earth.

The People

Close to 17 million people call Chile home. Almost all Chileans have **Amerindian** or European **ancestors**. Most Chileans are *mestizos*, or people of mixed background. When the Spanish came to Chile hundreds of years ago, many had children with the **native** peoples. **Immigrants** from France, Germany, and other European countries have also come to live in Chile. A small number of native groups still survive in the country. The largest of these groups is the Mapuche. Each of these groups speaks their own language. Most also speak Spanish, the official language of Chile.

Speak Spanish!

English	Spanish	How to say it
hello	hola	OH-lah
good-bye	adios	ah-dee-OHS
yes	sí	SEE
no	no	NOH
please	por favor	POHR fah-VOR
thank you	gracias	GRAH-see-uhs
friend (male)	amigo	ah-MEE-goh
friend (female)	amiga	ah-MEE-gah

Daily Life

About 9 out of every 10 Chileans live in cities. Most have houses or apartments. Early each morning, they take cars, buses, or the subway to work. They have a long lunch break and work late into the evening. Many Chileans do not go to bed until after midnight.

Most Chileans in the countryside live in houses on their farms. They rise with the sun and go to bed early after a long day of tending their crops and livestock. Many people use bikes or motorcycles to go to outdoor markets. Some farms are close enough to cities for families to shop at malls or supermarkets.

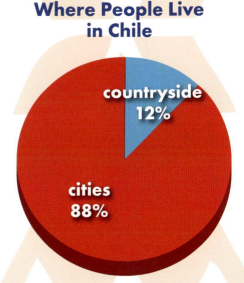

Where People Live in Chile

countryside 12%
cities 88%

Did you know?
Some Mapuche still build traditional wood houses with straw roofs.

Going to School

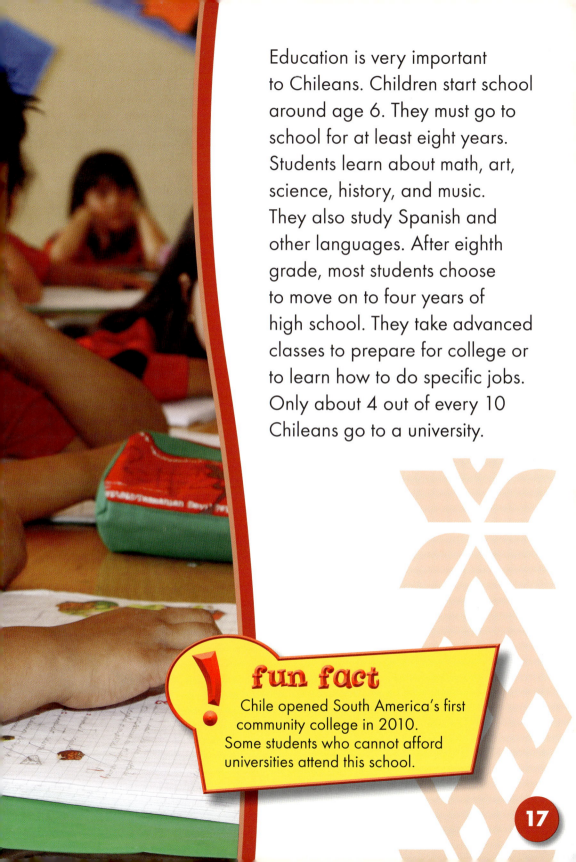

Education is very important to Chileans. Children start school around age 6. They must go to school for at least eight years. Students learn about math, art, science, history, and music. They also study Spanish and other languages. After eighth grade, most students choose to move on to four years of high school. They take advanced classes to prepare for college or to learn how to do specific jobs. Only about 4 out of every 10 Chileans go to a university.

fun fact

Chile opened South America's first community college in 2010. Some students who cannot afford universities attend this school.

Working

Where People Work in Chile

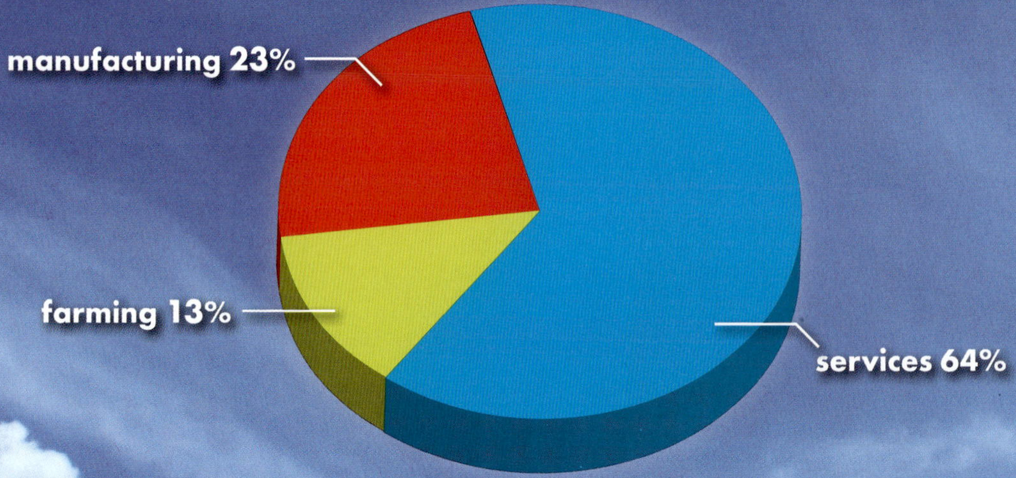

- manufacturing 23%
- farming 13%
- services 64%

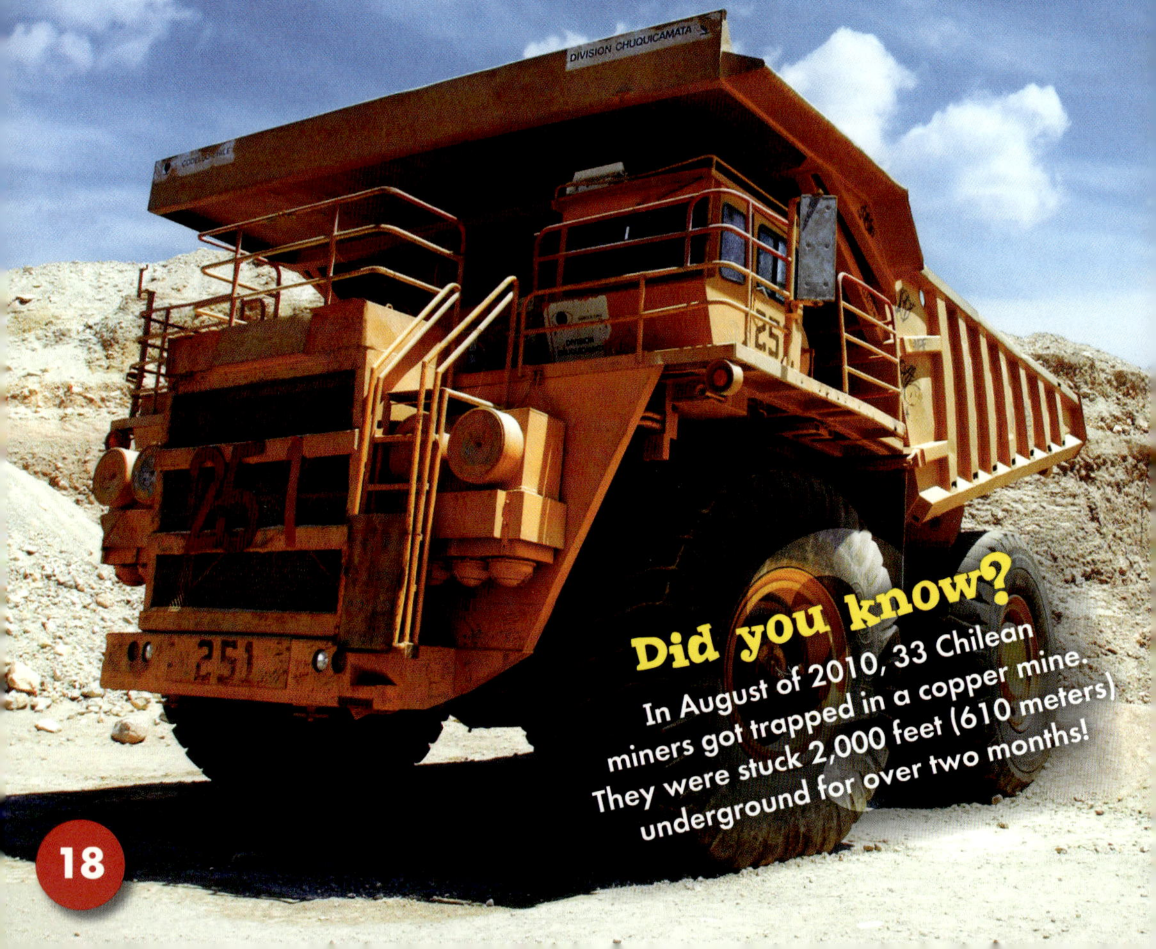

Did you know?
In August of 2010, 33 Chilean miners got trapped in a copper mine. They were stuck 2,000 feet (610 meters) underground for over two months!

Chileans in cities have different jobs than Chileans in the countryside. In cities, most people have **service jobs**. They work in schools, hospitals, banks, stores, and restaurants. Other Chileans work in factories. They make metals, food products, paper, and **textiles**. These products are sold all over the world.

Chileans in the countryside are miners, farmers, and fishermen. Miners dig up copper and other **minerals** from the earth. The Atacama Desert holds most of Chile's copper. Farmers grow avocados, grapes, corn, and other fruits and vegetables. Fishermen cast their nets into the water off Chile's long coast to catch seafood.

Playing

fun fact
Rodeo is Chile's national sport. In Chilean rodeo, riders compete in pairs. The riders, called *huasos*, work together to pin a bull against the wall of the arena.

Chileans enjoy a wide range of sports and outdoor activities. Their favorite sport is soccer. Thousands of fans pack the national stadium in Santiago to watch their favorite players compete. People also enjoy tennis, basketball, and golf.

The country's landscape offers many activities for Chileans. Families can hike and camp along nature trails. The Andes Mountains are perfect for skiing and snowboarding. Chile's beautiful beaches attract visitors who swim, surf, snorkel, and scuba dive. Sandboarding, which is similar to snowboarding, is popular on the **dunes** of the Atacama Desert.

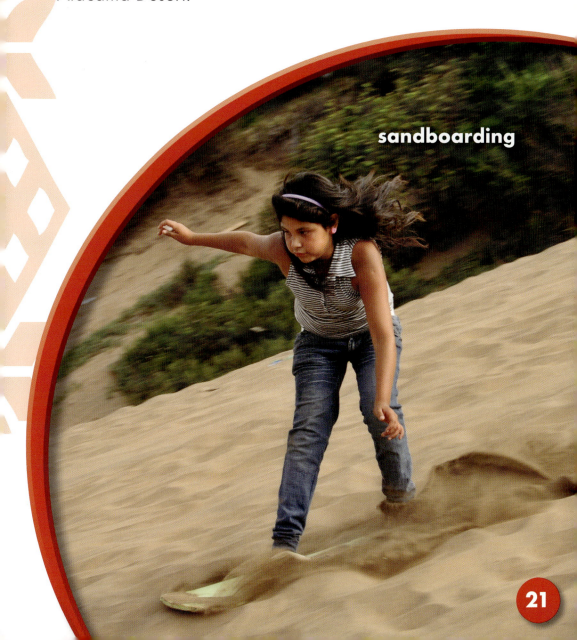

sandboarding

Food

Did you know?
Chileans enjoy outdoor barbeques called *asados*. They eat grilled meat with *pebre*, a spicy Chilean salsa.

Chile's long coast and rich farmland offer fresh seafood, meat, fruits, and vegetables. Most Chileans start the day with a simple breakfast of bread with coffee or tea. Lunch is the main meal of the day. *Humitas* are a popular food. Ground corn is mixed with onion and spices, then cooked in a husk. Stews called *cazuelas* are also common. To make them, meat and vegetables are mixed with rice or noodles in a broth. Many Chileans enjoy a corn and meat pie called *pastel de choclo*. Conger eel, or *congrio*, is a favorite seafood. Dinner is served late and is often just a sandwich. A popular dessert is an *alfajor*. It is a pastry layered with milk and coated in powdered sugar.

cazuela

congrio

Holidays

Easter

cueca

Most Chileans celebrate Christian holidays like Christmas and Easter. On Christmas, families feast and exchange gifts after attending church. The Sunday after Easter is the *Fiesta de Cuasimodo*. Priests and *huasos* parade through town. Hundreds of people follow them as they visit those who are too old or sick to attend church.

Chileans also celebrate many national holidays. September 18 is Independence Day. Many Chileans go to rodeos or dance the *cueca*, Chile's national dance. The next day is Armed Forces Day. It starts off with a huge parade in Santiago. These *fiestas patrias*, or national holiday celebrations, often last an entire week.

Easter Island

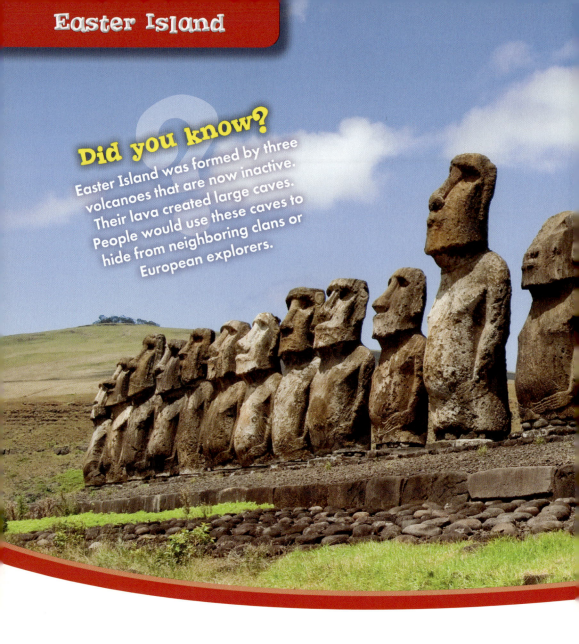

Did you know?
Easter Island was formed by three volcanoes that are now inactive. Their lava created large caves. People would use these caves to hide from neighboring clans or European explorers.

Easter Island lies about 2,200 miles (3,541 kilometers) off the coast of Chile. It became part of Chile in 1888. The first people to come to Easter Island were **Polynesians** who arrived around 400 CE. Over the last fifty years, Chileans have brought their own traditions to the island.

fun fact

Some statues on Easter Island are over 30 feet (9 meters) tall and weigh up to 160,000 pounds (72,575 kilograms).

Easter Island has about 900 statues that resemble human figures. Many people believe that these statues represent ancestors or other beings **sacred** to the Polynesians. Today, Easter Island blends the Polynesian and Chilean cultures. Chileans have embraced Easter Island and its people as a part of Chile.

Fast Facts About Chile

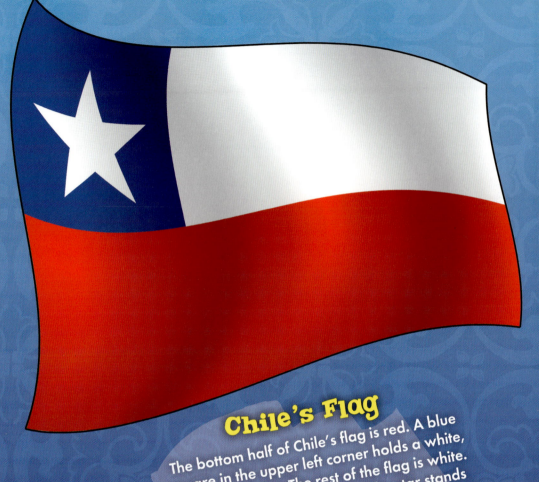

Chile's Flag

The bottom half of Chile's flag is red. A blue square in the upper left corner holds a white, five-pointed star. The rest of the flag is white. Blue represents the sky, and the star stands for honor. White represents the snow-covered Andes Mountains. Red is a symbol of Chile's independence.

Official Name: Republic of Chile

Area: 291,933 square miles (756,102 square kilometers); Chile is the 38th largest country in the world.

Capital City:	Santiago
Important Cities:	Arica, Antofagasta, Valparaíso, Viña del Mar, Concepción
Population:	16,888,760 (July 2011)
Official Language:	Spanish
National Holiday:	Independence Day (September 18)
Religions:	Christian (86.1%), Other (5.6%), None (8.3%)
Major Industries:	farming, fishing, forestry, mining, manufacturing, services
Natural Resources:	copper, iron ore, coal, oil, timber, natural gas, fish
Manufactured Products:	food products, wood products, cement, paper products, textiles, metal products, oil products
Farm Products:	avocados, grapes, apples, pears, onions, wheat, corn, oats, peaches, garlic, asparagus, beans, beef, poultry, wool
Unit of Money:	Chilean peso

Glossary

Amerindian—originally from North or South America

ancestors—relatives who lived long ago

cape—a point of land that sticks out into the sea

dunes—hills of sand

fjords—long, narrow inlets of the ocean between tall cliffs; the movement of glaciers makes fjords.

glaciers—massive sheets of ice that cover a large area of land

immigrants—people who leave one country to live in another country

minerals—elements found in nature; copper and iron ore are examples of minerals.

native—originally from a specific place

Polynesians—native peoples who live on Hawaii, Easter Island, and many other Pacific islands; *Polynesia* means "many islands."

rodents—small animals that gnaw on their food

sacred—holy, or very important to a culture or group of people

service jobs—jobs that perform tasks for people or businesses

textiles—fabrics or clothes that have been woven or knitted

tourists—people who are visiting a country

To Learn More

AT THE LIBRARY

Burgan, Michael. *Chile*. New York, N.Y.: Children's Press, 2010.

Ryan, Pam Muñoz. *The Dreamer.* New York, N.Y.: Scholastic Press, 2010.

Winter, Jane Kohen. *Chile*. New York, N.Y.: Benchmark Books, 2002.

ON THE WEB

Learning more about Chile is as easy as 1, 2, 3.

1. Go to www.factsurfer.com.

2. Enter "Chile" into the search box.

3. Click the "Surf" button and you will see a list of related Web sites.

With factsurfer.com, finding more information is just a click away.

Index

activities, 20, 21
Andes Mountains, 7, 21
Armed Forces Day, 25
Atacama Desert, 6, 10, 19, 21
Cape Horn, 7
capital (see Santiago)
climate, 6, 7
daily life, 14-15
Easter Island, 5, 26-27
education, 16-17
Fiesta de Cuasimodo, 25
food, 22-23
holidays, 24-25
housing, 14, 15
immigration, 13
Independence Day, 25
landscape, 6-9
languages, 13, 17
location, 4-5
Mapuche, 13, 15
peoples, 12-13, 15, 26, 27
Polynesians, 26, 27
Santiago, 4, 5, 25
seasons, 6
sports, 20, 21
Torres del Paine, 8-9
transportation, 14, 15
wildlife, 10-11
working, 18-19

The images in this book are reproduced through the courtesy of: P. Zonzei, front cover; Maisei Raman, front cover (flag), p. 28; Maggie Rosier, pp. 4-5; Gavin Hellier / Photolibrary, pp. 6, 14; Walter Bibikow / Photolibrary, p. 7; Robert Harding Images, pp. 8-9; Juan Martinez, pp. 10 (top & middle), 23 (left), 29 (bill); Michael Fogden / Photolibrary, p. 10 (bottom); Wildlife Bildagentur GmbH / Kimballstock, pp. 10-11; Blaine Harrington III / Alamy, p. 12; Bernard Foubert / Photolibrary, p. 15; Heiner Heine / Photolibrary, pp. 16-17; Benelux Benelux / Photolibrary, p. 18; M. Timothy O'Keefe / Alamy, p. 19 (left); Andy Christodolo / Alamy, p. 19 (right); Jochem Wijnands / Photolibrary, p. 20; Martin Bernetti / AFP / Getty, p. 21; Michael Taylor / Age Fotostock, p. 22; Ekaterina Pokrovsky, p. 23 (right); Barbara Boensch / Photolibrary, p. 24; Photolibrary, p. 25; Alberto Loyo, pp. 26-27.

Howard Elementary School LMC
657 W. Idlewild Court
Green Bay, WI 54303